THE CONSTITUTION
OF THE LATER ROMAN EMPIRE

THE CONSTITUTION
OF THE LATER ROMAN EMPIRE

CREIGHTON MEMORIAL LECTURE
DELIVERED AT UNIVERSITY COLLEGE, LONDON
12 NOVEMBER 1909

BY

J. B. BURY

REGIUS PROFESSOR OF MODERN HISTORY IN THE
UNIVERSITY OF CAMBRIDGE

Cambridge :
at the University Press
1910

CAMBRIDGE
UNIVERSITY PRESS

University Printing House, Cambridge CB2 8BS, United Kingdom

Published in the United States of America by Cambridge University Press, New York

Cambridge University Press is part of the University of Cambridge.

It furthers the University's mission by disseminating knowledge in the pursuit of education, learning and research at the highest international levels of excellence.

www.cambridge.org
Information on this title: www.cambridge.org/9781107680531

First published 1910
First paperback edition 2014

A catalogue record for this publication is available from the British Library

ISBN 978-1-107-68053-1 Paperback

THE CONSTITUTION OF THE LATER ROMAN EMPIRE

THE forms of government which are commonly classified as absolute monarchies have not received the same attention or been so carefully analysed as those forms which are known as republics and constitutional monarchies. There is a considerable literature on absolute monarchy considered theoretically, in connexion with the question of Divine Right, but the actual examples which history offers of this kind of government have not been the subject of a detailed comparative study. Montesquieu, for instance, treats them indiscriminately as despotisms. Probably the reason lies in the apparent simplicity of a constitution, by which the supreme power is exclusively vested in one man. When we say that the monarch's will is supreme, we may seem to

say all there is to be said. The Later Roman
Empire is an example of absolute monarchy,
and I propose to shew that so far as it is
concerned there is a good deal more to be
said.

The term absolute monarchy is applied
in contradistinction to limited or constitutional monarchy. I understand the former
to mean that the whole legislative, judicial,
and executive powers of the state are vested
in the monarch, and there is no other independent and concurrent authority[1]. The
latter means that besides the so-called
monarch there are other political bodies
which possess an independent and effective
authority of their own, and share in the
sovran power. These terms, absolute and
constitutional monarchy, are unsatisfactory,
from a logical point of view. For they group
together these two forms of government as
subdivisions of the class monarchy, implying
or suggesting that they have much more real
affinity to one another than either has to
other constitutions. This is evidently untrue:

a constitutional monarchy is far more closely allied to a republic like France than to an absolute monarchy like Russia. The English constitution, for instance, in which legislation is effected by the consent of three independent organs, the Crown, the Lords, and the Commons, might be described more correctly as a triarchy than as a monarchy; and it seems to be unfortunate that monarchy should have come to be used, quite unnecessarily, as a synonym for kingship. "Limited monarchy," as Austin said long ago, "is not monarchy[2]"; monarchy properly so-called is, simply and solely, absolute monarchy. We have however an alternative term, "autocracy," which involves no ambiguities, and might, I venture to think, be advantageously adopted as the technical term for this form of government in constitutional discussions. And "autocracy" has a special advantage over "absolute monarchy." Autocracies are not all alike, in respect to the power actually exercised by the autocrat. Although not limited by any bodies possessing an independent authority, he may be limited effectually in other ways. Now we can properly speak of more or less limited autocracies, whereas it is an impropriety of language to speak of more or less absolute monarchies, as "absolute" admits of no degrees.

Originally, and during the first three centuries of its existence, the Roman Empire was theoretically a republic. The Senate co-existed with the Emperor, as a body invested with an authority independent of his; but the functions which it exercised by virtue of that authority were surrendered one by one; it became more and more dependent on him; and by the end of the third century the fiction of a second power in the state was dropped altogether, although the Senate was not abolished[3]. From that time forward, under the system established by Diocletian and Constantine, until the fall of the Empire in the fifteenth century, the government was simply and undisguisedly an autocracy.

Now one broad distinction between autocracies may be found in the mode of accession to the throne. The sovranty may be hereditary or it may be elective. If it is elective, the sovranty is derived from the electors who, when the throne is vacant, exercise an independent and sovran authority in electing a new monarch. If it is hereditary, if the right of the autocrat depends entirely and indefeasibly on his birth, then we may say that his sovranty is underived; the succession is automatic, and there is no moment at which any other person or persons than the monarch can perform an act of sovran authority such as is implied in the election of a sovran. This difference may involve, as we shall see, important consequences.

In the case of the Roman Empire, the Imperial dignity continued to be elective, as it had been from the beginning, and the method of election remained the same. When the throne was vacant a new Emperor was chosen by the Senate and the army. The initiative might be taken either by the Senate or by the army, and both methods were recognised as equally valid. It was of course only a portion of the army that actually chose an Emperor,—for instance, if the choice were made in Constantinople, the guard regiments; but such a portion was regarded as for this purpose representing all the troops which were scattered over the Empire. The appointment did not take the formal shape of what we commonly understand by election. If the soldiers took the initiative, they simply proclaimed the man they wanted. If the choice was made by the Senate, the procedure might be more deliberate, but there seems to have been no formal casting of votes, and the essential act was the proclamation[4]. It sufficed that one of these bodies should proclaim an Emperor to establish his title to the sovranty; it only remained for the other body to concur; and the inauguration was formally completed when the people of Constantinople had also acclaimed him in the Hippodrome—a formality always observed and reminiscent of the fact that the inhabitants of the new capital of Constantine had succeeded to the position of the old *populus Romanus*[5].

The part which the Senate played in the appointment of an Emperor, whether by choosing him or by ratifying the choice of the army, is constitutionally important. The Senate or *Synklêtos* of New Rome was a very different body from the old Senatus Romanus. It was a small council consisting of persons who belonged to it by virtue of administrative offices to which they were appointed by the Emperor. In fact, the old Senate had coalesced with the Consistorium or Imperial council, and in consequence the new Senate had a double aspect. So long as there was a reigning Emperor, it acted as consistorium or advisory council of the sovran, but when there was an interval between two reigns, it resumed the independent authority which had lain in abeyance and performed functions which it had inherited from the early Senate.

But it was not only when the throne was vacant that it could perform such functions.

The right of election might be exercised by the Senate and the army at any time. It was a principle of state-law in the Early Empire that the people which made the Emperor could also unmake him, and this principle continued in force under the autocracy. There was no formal process of deposing a sovran, but the members of the community had the means of dethroning him, if his government failed to give satisfaction, by proclaiming a new Emperor; and if anyone so proclaimed obtained sufficient support from the army, Senate, and people, the old Emperor was compelled to vacate the throne, retiring into a monastery, losing his eyesight, or suffering death, according to the circumstances of the situation or the temper of his supplanter; while the new Emperor was regarded as the legitimate monarch from the day on which he was proclaimed; the proclamation was taken as the legal expression of the general will. If he had not a sufficient following to render the proclamation effective and was suppressed, he was treated as a rebel; but during the struggle and before the catastrophe, the fact that a portion of the army had proclaimed him gave him a presumptive constitutional status, which the event might either confirm or annul. The method of deposition was in fact revolution, and we are accustomed to regard revolution as something essentially unconstitutional, an appeal from law to force; but under the Imperial system, it was not unconstitutional; the government was, to use an expression of Mommsen, "an autocracy tempered by the legal right of revolution."

Thus the sovranty of the Roman autocrat was delegated to him by the community, as represented by the Senate, and the army, and, we may add, the people of Constantinople[6]. The symbol of the sovranty thus delegated was the diadem, which was definitely introduced by Constantine. The Emperor wore other insignia, such as the purple robe and the red boots, but the diadem was preeminently the symbol and expression of the autocracy. The dress only represented the Imperator or commander-in-chief of the army, and no formalities were connected with its assumption. It was otherwise with the crown, which in the Persian Kingdom, from which it was borrowed, was placed on the king's head by the High-priest of the Magian religion. In theory, the Imperial crown should be imposed by a representative of those who conferred the sovran authority which it symbolized. And in the fourth century we find the Prefect, Sallustius Secundus, crowning Valentinian I, in whose election he had taken the most prominent part. But the Emperors seem to have felt some hesitation in thus receiving the diadem from the hands of a subject; and the selection of one magnate for this high office of conferring the symbol of sovranty was likely to cause enmity and jealousy. Yet a formality was considered necessary. In the fifth century, the difficulty was overcome in a clever and tactful way. The duty of coronation was assigned to the Patriarch of Constantinople. In discharging this office, the Patriarch was not envied by the secular magnates because he could not be their rival, and his ecclesiastical position relieved the Emperor from all embarrassment in receiving the diadem from a subject. There is some evidence, though it is not above suspicion, that this plan was adopted at the coronation of Marcian in A.D. 450, but it seems certain that his successor Leo was crowned by the Patriarch in A.D. 457. Henceforward this was the regular practice. In the thirteenth century we find Theodore II postponing his coronation until the Patriarchal throne, which happened to be vacant, was filled. But although it was the regular and desirable form of coronation, it was never regarded as indispensable for the autocrat's legitimate inauguration. The last of the East Roman Emperors, Constantine Palaeologus, was not crowned by the Patriarch; he was crowned by a layman[7]. This fact that coronation by the Patriarch was not constitutionally necessary, though it was the usual custom, is significant. For it shows that the Patriarch, in performing the ceremony, was not representing the Church. It is possible that the idea of committing the office to him was suggested by the Persian coronations which were performed by the High-priest, but the significance was not the same. The chief of the Magians acted as the representative of the Persian religion, the Patriarch acted as the representative of the State[8]. For if he had specially represented the Church, it is clear that his co-operation could never have been dispensed with. In other words, no new constitutional theory or constitutional requirement was introduced by the assignment of the privilege of crowning Emperors to the Patriarch. It did not mean that the consent of the Church was formally necessary to the inauguration of the sovran.

I will make this point still more evident presently in connexion with another important feature of the constitution to which we now come. If you look down the roll of Emperors, you will find that only a minority

of them were actually elected in the ways
I have described. In most cases, when an
Emperor died, the throne was not vacant,
for generally he had a younger colleague,
who had already been invested with the
Imperial dignity, so that no new election was
necessary. This practice[9] by which a reigning Emperor could appoint his successor
modified the elective principle. The Emperor
used to devolve the succession upon his son,
if he had one; so that son constantly succeeded father, and the history of the Roman
Empire is marked by a series of hereditary
dynasties. The constitution thus combined
the elective and the hereditary principles;
a device was found for securing the advan-
tages of hereditary succession, and obviating
its disadvantages by preserving the principle
of election. The chief advantage of hereditary monarchy is that it avoids the danger
of domestic troubles and civil war which are
likely to occur when the throne is elective,
and there are two rival candidates. Its chief
disadvantage is that the supreme power in

the State will inevitably devolve sometimes upon a weak and incapable ruler. The result of the mixture of the two principles, the dynastic and the elective, was that there were far fewer incapable sovrans than if the dynastic succession had been exclusively valid, and fewer struggles for power than if every change of ruler had meant an election. It would be interesting to trace, if we had the material, how the inhabitants of the Empire became more and more attached to the idea of legitimacy—the idea that the children of an Emperor had a constitutional right to the supreme power.   We can see at least that this feeling grew very strong under the long rule of the Macedonian dynasty; it is illustrated by the political *rôle* which the Empress Zoe, an utterly incompetent and depraved old woman, was allowed to play because she was the daughter of Constantine VIII.   But the fact remained that although a father invariably raised his eldest son, and sometimes younger sons too, to the rank of Augustus, the son became Emperor by virtue of his father's will and not by virtue of his birth. The Emperor was not in any way bound to devolve the succession upon his son[10]. Now what I ask you to observe is that when a reigning sovran created a second Emperor, whether his son or anyone else, there was no election. The Senate, the army, and the people expressed their joy and satisfaction, in the ceremonies which attended the creation, but the creation was entirely the act of the Emperor. The constitutional significance is evident. The autocratic powers conferred upon an Emperor by his election included the right of devolving the Imperial dignity upon others. It was part of his sovranty to be able to create a colleague who was potentially another sovran.

This difference between the appointment of an Emperor when the throne is vacant and the appointment of an Emperor as colleague when the throne is occupied is clearly and significantly expressed by the difference between the coronation acts in the two cases. In the former case the act is performed by a representative of the electors, almost always the Patriarch; in the latter case it is regularly performed by the reigning Emperor. It is he who, possessing the undivided sovranty, confers the Imperial dignity and therefore with his own hands delivers its symbol. Sometimes indeed he commits the office of coronation to the Patriarch, but the Patriarch is then acting simply as his delegate[11]. This difference is a confirmation of the view that the Patriarch, in discharging the duty of coronation, acts as a representative of the electors, and not of the Church. For if the coronation had been conceived as a religious act, it must have been performed in the same way, in all cases, by the chief minister of the Church.

But now you may ask, is the term autocracy or the term monarchy strictly applicable to the Empire? Monarchy and autocracy mean the sovran rule of one man alone, but, as we have just seen, the Emperor generally had a colleague. Both in the early and in the later Empire, there were constantly two

Emperors, sometimes more. In the tenth century, for instance, in the reign of Romanus I, there were as many as five—each of them an Augustus, each a Basileus[12]. This practice is derived from the original collegial character of the proconsular Imperium and the tribunician power, on which Augustus based his authority. But, although the Roman Imperium or Basileia was collegial, the sovranty was not divided. When there were two Emperors only one exercised the sovran power and governed the State; his colleague was subordinate, and simply enjoyed the dignity and the expectation of succession. Though his name appeared in legislative acts and his effigy on coins, and though he shared in all the Imperial honours, he was a sleeping partner. With one exception, which I will notice presently, the only cases of Imperial colleagues exercising concurrent sovranty were in the period from Diocletian to the death of Julius Nepos, when the Empire was territorially divided. Diocletian and Maximian, for instance, the sons of Constan-

B. 2

tine, Arcadius and Honorius, were severally
monarchs in their own dominions. But except in the case of territorial division, the
supreme power was exercised by one man,
and monarchy is therefore a right description of the constitution. In the reign of
Constantine IV, the soldiers demanded that
the Emperor should crown his two brothers.
"We believe in the Trinity," they cried, "and
we would have three Emperors." But this
must not be interpreted as a demand that
each member of the desired Imperial trinity
should exercise sovran authority. Such a
joint sovranty was never tried except in one
case, and a clear distinction was drawn between
the Basileus who governed and the Basileus
who did not govern. The exceptional case
was the peculiar one of two Empresses, who
ruled conjointly for a short time in the eleventh
century. I will mention this case again, in
a few minutes, when I come to speak of the
position of Empresses.

And here I must dwell for a moment on
the name *Basileus* and another Greek name

Autokrator, which were employed to designate the Emperor. In the early Empire, Basileus was used in the East and especially in Egypt, where Augustus was regarded as the successor of the Ptolemies, but it was not used officially by the Emperors; it was not the Greek for Imperator. The Greek word adopted to translate Imperator was Autokrator, and this is the term always used in Imperial Greek inscriptions. By the fourth century Basileus had come into universal use in the Greek-speaking parts of the Empire; it was the regular term used by Greek writers; but it was not yet accepted as an official title. Nor was it adopted officially till the seventh century in the reign of Heraclius. It has been pointed out by Bréhier[13] that the earliest official act in which an Emperor entitles himself Basileus is a law of Heraclius of the year 629. In the earlier diplomas of his reign he uses the old traditional form Autokrator. Bréhier, however, has failed to see the reason of this change of style, but the significant date A.D. 629 supplies the explanation. In that year Heraclius completed the conquest of Persia. Now, the Persian king was the only foreign monarch to whom the Roman Emperors conceded the title Basileus; except the Abyssinian king, who hardly counted. So long as there was a great independent Basileus outside the Roman Empire, the Emperors refrained from adopting a title which would be shared by another monarch. But as soon as that monarch was reduced to the condition of a dependent vassal and there was no longer a concurrence, the Emperor signified the event by assuming officially the title which had for several centuries been applied to him unofficially. The Empire was extremely conservative in forms and usages; changes were slow in official documents, they were slower still in the coinage. It is not till more than a century later that Basileus begins to be adopted by the mint. By this change Basileus became the official equivalent of Imperator; it took the place of Autokrator; and it was now possible for Autokrator to come into its own and express its full etymological significance. Thus we find a strongly marked tendency in later times to apply the term specially to the Basileus who was the actual ruler. Though he and his colleague might be acclaimed jointly as Autokrators; yet Autokrator is distinctly used to express the plenitude of despotic power which was exercised by the senior Emperor alone[14]. Thus we may say that in early times Basileus was the pregnant title which expressed that full monarchical authority which the system of Augustus aimed at disguising, and Autokrator was simply the equivalent of the republican title Imperator; while in later times the *rôles* of the two titles were reversed, and Autokrator became the pregnant title, expressing the fulness of authority which the familiar Basileus no longer emphasized.

Before we leave this part of our subject, a word must be said about the rights of women to exercise autocracy. From the foundation of the Empire the title of Augusta had been conferred on the wives of Emperors, and we find in early times the mothers of minors, like Agrippina and Julia Domna, exercising political power. But this power was always exercised in the name of their sons. At the beginning of the fifth century the Augusta Pulcheria presides over the government which acted for her brother Theodosius II while he was a minor. On his death without children, it is recognised that although she cannot govern alone, she nevertheless has a right to have a voice in the election of a new Emperor, and the situation is met by her nominal marriage with Marcian. Similarly, forty years later, when Zeno dies without a son, his wife, the Augusta Ariadne, has, by general consent, the decisive voice in selecting her husband's successor; her choice falls on Anastasius, and he is elected. But it is not she who confers the Imperial authority on Anastasius, it is the Senate and army, who elect him, in accordance with her wishes. In the following century, the political importance of Empresses is augmented by the exceptional

positions occupied by Theodora the consort
of Justinian, and Sophia the consort of Justin
II. But so far although an Empress may
act as regent for a minor[15], may intervene in
an Imperial election, may receive honours
suggesting that she is her husband's colleague
rather than consort, she never exercises independent sovran power, she is never, in the
later sense of the word, an Autokrator.
Passing on to the close of the eighth century,
we come to the Empress Irene, the Athenian
lady who is famous as the first restorer of
Image-worship. When her husband died, her
son Constantine was too young to rule, and
she governed in the same way as Pulcheria
had governed for Theodosius. When Constantine was old enough to govern himself,
Irene was unwilling to retire into the back-
ground, and although the son succeeded
in holding the power in his own hands for
some years, the mother was continually in-
triguing against him. The struggle ended in
her triumph. She caused her son to be
blinded, and for five years she reigned alone

with full sovran powers as Autokrator.   This
was a considerable constitutional innovation,
and the official style of her diplomas illustrates, in an interesting way, that it was felt
as such.   She was, of course, always spoken
of as the Empress, but in her official acts she
is styled not "Irene the Empress" but "Irene
the Emperor" (*Basileus*)[16].   It was felt that
only an Emperor could legislate, and so the
legal fiction of her masculinity was adopted.

It was said in Western Europe, for the
purpose of justifying the Imperial claim of
Charles the Great, that the sovranty of the
Empire could not devolve on a woman, and
that Irene's tenure of power was really an
interregnum; but the Byzantines never admitted this constitutional doctrine.   Nevertheless they had a strong objection to the
régime of women, except in the capacity of
regents, and the precedent established by
Irene was repeated only in the case of Zoe
and Theodora, the two nieces of Basil II.
We find each of these ladies exercising the
sovran authority alone for brief periods, and

we also find them ruling together. This is the instance, which I mentioned already, of the experiment of government by two autocrats. Their joint rule might have been protracted, if they had been in harmony, but Zoe was extremely jealous of Theodora, and in order to oust her she took a husband, who immediately assumed the autocratic authority, and Zoe fell back into the subordinate position of a consort.

We may now pass to the consideration of the nature and amplitude of the Imperial supremacy. The act of proclamation conferred his sovran powers upon the Emperor. In early days the Imperial powers were defined explicitly by a law, the *lex de imperio*. We have the text of the law which was passed for Vespasian. But the practice of passing it anew on the accession of a new Emperor was discontinued, and under the autocracy, when all the legislative, judicial and executive powers were vested in the autocrat, there was no reason to define what those powers were. In the sixth century however, in the legislation of Justinian, it is recognised that by the *lex de imperio* the people transferred its sovranty to the Emperor. In the eighth century we may be pretty sure that no one from the Emperor downwards had ever heard of the *lex de imperio*[17]. But although there was no constitution of this kind defining or limiting the monarch's functions, I will proceed to shew that his power, legally unlimited, was subject to limitations which must be described as constitutional.

For his legislative and administrative acts, the monarch was responsible to none, except to Heaven; there was no organ in the state that had a right to control him; so that his government answers to our definition of autocracy. But when the monarch is appointed by any body or bodies in the state, the electors can impose conditions on him at the time of election, and thus there is the possibility of limiting his power. In other words, an elective autocracy, like the Roman Empire, is liable to the imposition of limitations. The case of the Emperor Anastasius I is in point. The Senate required from him an oath that he would administer the Empire conscientiously and not visit offences upon anyone with whom he had had a quarrel. This exhibits the principle, which was constantly and chiefly applied for the purpose of preventing a new Emperor from making ecclesiastical innovations.

It was a recognised condition of eligibility to the throne that the candidate should be a Christian, and an orthodox Christian. The latest pagan Emperor was Julian. After him it would have been virtually impossible for a pagan to rule at Constantinople. After the Council of Constantinople in A.D. 381, which crushed the Arian heresies, it would have been impossible for an Arian to wear the diadem. This was expressly recognised in the situation which ensued on the death of Theodosius II. The most prominent man at the moment was Aspar, but he was an Arian, and on that account alone his elevation was considered out of the question. Up to that period it may be said that such conditions of faith were political rather than constitutional; but when the coronation ceremony was attended with religious forms, we may say that Christianity was coming to be considered a constitutional condition of eligibility. By religious forms, I do not mean the part which the Patriarch played in the act of coronation, which, as we have seen, had no ecclesiastical significance, but other parts of the ceremony, such as prayers, which were introduced in the fifth century. It was at the accession of Anastasius I that a religious declaration was first required from an Emperor. Anastasius was with good reason suspected of heterodoxy; he was in fact a monophysite. He was not asked to make any personal confession of faith, but at the Patriarch's demand, he signed a written oath that he would maintain the existing ecclesiastical settlement unimpaired and introduce no novelty in the Church. We are ignorant whether such a written declaration was formally required at all subsequent elections; probably not; but it was, we know, imposed

in a number of cases where there was reason
to suspect a new Emperor of heretical ten-
dencies. Ultimately, we cannot say at what
time, this practice crystallised into the shape
of a regular coronation oath, in which the
monarch confesses and confirms the decrees
of the Seven Ecumenical Councils and of the
local synods, and the privileges of the Church,
and vows to be a mild ruler and to abstain as
far as possible from punishments of death and
mutilation[18].

The fact that such capitulations could be
and were imposed at the time of election,
even though the Emperor's obligation to
submit to them was moral rather than legal,
means that the autocracy was subject to
limitations and was limited. But apart from
such definite capitulations, the monarch's
power was restricted by unwritten principles
of government which bound him as much as
the unwritten part of the English constitution
binds our king and government. The autocrat
was the supreme legislator; personally he
was above the laws, *solutus legibus*[19]; there

was no tribunal before which he could be summoned; but he was bound by the principles and the forms of the law which was the great glory of Roman civilisation [20]. He could modify laws, he could make new laws; but no Emperor ever questioned the obligation of conforming his acts to the law or presumed to assert that he could set it aside. Although theoretically above the law, he was at the same time bound by it, *alligatus legibus*, as Theodosius II expressly acknowledges [21]. Basil I, in a legal handbook, explicitly affirms the obligation of the Emperor to maintain not only the Scriptures and the canons of the Seven Councils, but also the Roman laws. And the laws embraced the institutions. Though changing circumstances led to adaptations and alterations, the Byzantine conservatism, which is almost proverbial and is often exaggerated, attests the strength of the unwritten limitations which always restrained the Imperial autocracy.

The Senate, too, though it had no share

in the sovranty, might operate as a check on the sovran's actions. For there were various political matters which the Emperor was bound by custom to lay before it. We have not the material for enumerating what those matters were, but among the most important were questions of peace and war and the conclusion of treaties. The Senate would obediently concur in the views of a strong sovran, and probably its meetings were generally of a purely formal nature, but it is significant that in the case of a weak Emperor (Michael I) we find the Senate opposing the autocrat's wishes and the autocrat bowing to their opinion[22].

It is implied in what I have said that the Church represented a limit on the Emperor's power. From the ninth century onward, the Decrees of the Seven Councils were an unalterable law which no Emperor could touch[23]. At the same time, the relation of the state to the Church, of which I must now speak, illustrates the amplitude of his power. The Byzantine Church is the most important

example in history of a State-Church. Its
head was the Emperor. He was considered
the delegate of God in a sphere which
included the ecclesiastical as well as the
secular order. The Patriarch of Constantinople was his minister of the department of religion, and though the usual forms
of episcopal election were observed, was
virtually appointed by him. It was the
Emperor who convoked the Ecumenical
Councils, and it was the Emperor who pre-
sided at them either in person or, if he
did not care to suffer the boredom of theological debates, represented by some of his
secular ministers[24]. Canonical decrees passed
at councils did not become obligatory till
they were confirmed by the Emperor; and
the Emperors issued edicts and laws relating
to purely ecclesiastical affairs, quite inde-
pendently of Councils. The Patriarch Menas
asserted in the reign of Justinian that nothing
should be done in the Church contrary to
the Emperor's will, and Justinian, who was
the incarnation of sacerdotal monarchy, was

acclaimed as High-Priest Basileus (ἀρχιερεὺς βασιλεύς). It is true that the voices of prominent ecclesiastics were raised from time to time protesting that ecclesiastical matters lay outside the domain of secular authority and advocating the complete freedom of the Church. But this idea, of which Theodore of Studion was the latest champion, never gained ground; it was definitely defeated in the ninth century, and the Emperor continued to hold the position of a Christian caliph. Thus the theory of State and Church in the Eastern Empire is conspicuously contrasted with the theory which in Western Europe was realised under Innocent III. In both cases Church and State are indivisible, but in the West the Church is the State, whereas in the East it is a department which the Emperor directs. In the West we have a theocracy; the Church represented by the Pope claims to possess the supreme authority in temporal as well as spiritual affairs. In the East relations are reversed; instead of a theocracy, we have what has been called

B.   3

caesaropapism. A papalist writer, who en-
deavours to demonstrate the Pope's universal
supremacy, remarks that in point of juris-
diction a layman might be Pope; all the
powers and rights of a Pope, in spiritual as
well as secular affairs, would be conferred
upon him by election[25]. This hypothesis of
Agostino Trionfo was realised in the Eastern
Empire.

There were occasional struggles between
the Emperor and the Patriarch, usually
caused by an attempt on the Emperor's part
to introduce, for political reasons, some new
doctrine which the Patriarch considered
inconsistent with the Decrees of the Councils
or the Scriptures. In such cases the Patriarch
was defending the constitution against innovation; he was not disputing the Emperor's
position as head of the Church. And in such
cases the usual result was that the Patriarch
either yielded or was deposed, the Emperor
had his way, and the orthodox doctrine was
not reinstated until another Emperor reversed the acts of his predecessor. Some

Patriarchs might suggest that the Emperor, not being an expert in theology, ought not to interfere in matters of doctrine; but the normal relations were generally accepted as fundamental and constitutional.

The Patriarch had indeed one weapon which he might use against his sovran—the weapon of excommunication. He might refuse, and direct his clergy to refuse, to communicate with the Emperor. It was a weapon to which recourse was seldom taken. Another means of exerting power which the Patriarch possessed was due to the part which he took in the coronation. He might make terms with the new Emperor before he crowned him. Thus the Patriarch Polyeuktos forced John Tzimiskes to consent to abrogate a law which required the Imperial approbation of candidates for ecclesiastical offices before they were elected.

The constitutional theory which I have delineated is implied in the actual usages from which I have drawn it; but it was never formulated. Constitutional questions did not arise, and no lawyer or historian expounded the basis or the limits of the sovran power. In fact, the constitution was not differentiated in men's consciousness from the whole body of laws and institutions. They did not analyse the assumptions implied in their practice, and the only idea they entertained, which can be described as a constitutional theory, does not agree, though it may be conciliated, with the theory that I have sketched. If you had asked a Byzantine Emperor what was the basis of his autocracy and by what right he exercised it, he would not have told you that it had been committed to him by the Senate, the army, or the people; he would have said that he derived his sovranty directly from God. I could produce a great deal of evidence to illustrate this view, but it will be enough to refer to the words of the Emperor Basil I in his Advice to his son Leo : "You received the Empire from God"; "You received the crown from God by my hand[26]." Such a doctrine of the monarch's divine right naturally tended to reflect a new significance on the part which the Patriarch played in the Emperor's inauguration. But it found an explicit symbolic expression in the new custom of unction, which perhaps was practised (though opinions differ on this point)[27] as early as the ninth century. In crowning, the Patriarch expressed the will of the state; in anointing, the will of the Deity. This theory, logically developed, implies the view which Dante expresses in his *De Monarchia*, that the Electors when they choose the Emperor are merely voicing the choice of the Deity. It was quite in accordance with the prevailing religious sentiments; it enhanced the Emperor's authority by representing that authority as a divine gift, and perhaps it sometimes enhanced his sense of responsibility. But although calculated to place the sovran above criticism, this theory of divine right did not affect the actual working of the constitutional tradition which determined the appointment of Emperors and the limitations of their power.

Its chief interest lies in its relation to the political theories which were evolved in the Middle Ages in Western Europe. It has been observed by Mr Bryce[28], as a striking contrast between the Eastern and Western Empires, that, while the West was fertile in conceptions and theories, displaying abundant wealth of creative imagination, in the East men did not trouble themselves to theorize about the Empire at all. The inspiration, in the West, came in the first place from the fact that the Holy Roman Empire was always an ideal, never fully realised, "a dream" (to use Mr Bryce's words), "half theology and half poetry." The Eastern Roman Empire, on the other hand, was always an actual fact, adequate to its own conception; there it was,—there was no mistake about its being here and now; there was much in it to cause pride, there was nothing to stir imagination. In the second place, there was no need, in the Eastern Empire, to evolve theories, as nothing was in dispute. In the West a great constitutional question arose, of far-reaching practical importance, touching the relations of the two rival authorities, the Pope and the Emperor. It was to solve the political problem set by their rival pretensions that Dante wrote his *De Monarchia*, William of Ockham his *Dialogue*, Marsilius of Padua his *Defensor pacis*. In the East no such problem arose, inasmuch as the Emperor was recognised as the head of the Church, and there was therefore no stimulus to evolve political theories. Yet if a similar problem or need had arisen, I cannot help thinking that the medieval Greeks, though they were incapable of producing a Dante, would have proved themselves not less ingenious than Western thinkers in political speculation. But it is instructive to observe that the claim of the Eastern Emperor to derive his sovranty directly from God is the same theory of Divine Right which was asserted by the Western Imperialist writers. Dante affirmed this theory most forcibly; William of Ockham and Marsilius affirmed it too, but they tempered it by the view that the Empire was originally derived from the people, thus combining, as it were, the Divine pretensions of the later autocrats of Constantinople with the democratic origin of sovranty which is asserted in the lawbooks of Justinian.

I have endeavoured to shew how the autocracy of the later Roman Empire was a limited autocracy. Every autocracy, every government, has of course natural limitations. The action of the monarch is limited by public opinion; there will always be some point beyond which he is afraid to venture in defying public opinion. It is also limited by the fact that he has to employ human instruments, and their personal views and qualities may modify or compromise or thwart the execution of his will. Further, if he rules over a highly organized society, he may be restrained from sweeping measures by the knowledge that such changes will involve other consequences which he does not desire[29]. These natural limitations affect all autocracies, all governments, in various modes and degrees. But apart from them, the

Roman autocracy had definite restrictions which must be described as constitutional[30]. In what is miscalled a limited monarchy, the king may have legal rights which it would be unconstitutional to exercise. The action of the English crown, for instance, is restricted not merely by the statutory limits, such as are imposed on it by the Bill of Rights or the Act of Settlement, but by unwritten constitutional usage, which is obligatory. In the same way the action of the Roman autocrat was limited by a tradition and usage which were felt by him and by the community to be absolutely binding. The sanctions in the two cases are different. An English king is hindered from exceeding the constitutional bounds of his authority by the power which Parliament possesses of bringing the government to a standstill, as it can do by refusing to grant supplies or to pass the Mutiny Act. The more powerful Roman monarch was forced to conform to the institutions, customs, and traditions of his society by the more drastic sanction of deposition. The Russian

autocrat, Peter the Great, abolished the
Patriarchate of Moscow; it would have been
an impossibility for the Roman Emperor to
abolish the Patriarchate of Constantinople
or to introduce any serious change in the
organization of the Church.   The integrity
of the Church was indeed secured against
him not merely by this moral force, but by
capitulations which, in consequence of the
elective character of the monarchy, he could
be obliged to swear to at his accession and
which were finally embodied in a coronation
oath.   Here there was a religious sanction
superadded.

The limitations tended to maintain the
conservative character for which Byzantium
is often reproached, and were in fact one of
the results of that conservatism.   They were
efficacious, because the autocrat himself was
usually imbued deeply with this conservative
spirit, being a child of his age and civilisation; whilst the complex and elaborate
machinery, furnishing the channels through
which he had to act, was a powerful check on

his freedom. It must, I think, be admitted that the autocracy of the Eastern Empire suited the given conditions, and probably worked better than any other system that could have been devised. The government was not arbitrary, and the evils from which the subjects of the Empire suffered were due (apart from the calamities of war) to economic ignorance and bad finance, such as prevailed everywhere alike in the ancient and the middle ages, and would have pressed as heavily under any other form of government. The freedom and absence of formality in the method of appointing the sovran made it possible to meet different situations in different ways; and if we examine the roll of Emperors from Constantine the Great in the fourth to Manuel Comnenus in the twelfth century, we must admit that the constitution secured, with a few dark but short intervals, a succession of able and hard-working rulers such as cannot, I think, be paralleled in the annals of any other state during so long a period.

NOTES

[1] This differs somewhat from Sidgwick's definition, in *Development of European Polity*, p. 10 : "What is meant by calling him [an Absolute Monarch] 'absolute' is that there is no established constitutional authority—no human authority that his subjects habitually obey as much as they obey him—which can legitimately resist him or call him to account."

[2] *Lectures on Jurisprudence*, i. 241 (ed. 1885).

[3] The *Roman* Senate however seems to have retained some nominal sovranty ; for under the *régime* of Theodoric it had the power, like the Emperor, *constituere leges* (a power which Theodoric did not possess). Cp. Cassiodorus, *Variae*, 6, 4, § 1, 2 (p. 177, ed. Mommsen).

[4] This (ἀναγόρευσις) is the technical word applied to the whole procedure of inauguration.

[5] In the early Empire, the Roman people took the initiative in proclaiming Pertinax ; they forced the Praetorians to proclaim him ; but undoubtedly it was the proclamation of the latter that conferred the Imperium. In the later Empire we find a section of the people of Constantinople taking the initiative in proclaiming the nephews of Anastasius, on the occasion of the Nika revolt against Justinian.

[6] Cp. for instance Leo Diaconus, ii. 12, where Polyeuktos says that the sons of Romanus II were proclaimed Emperors "by us (the Senate) and the whole people."

[7] Nicephorus Bryennios, who was proclaimed Emperor in the reign of Michael VII (11th cent.) and was suppressed, placed the diadem on his own head, Anna Comnena, *Alexiad* i. 4.

[8] This is brought out by W. Sickel in his important article *Das byzantinische Krönungsrecht bis zum* 10 *Jahrhundert,* in the *Byzantinische Zeitschrift,* vii. 511 sqq. (1898), to which I must acknowledge my obligations. For the details of the coronation ceremonies see F. E. Brightman's article in the *Journal of Theological Studies,* ii. 359 sqq. (1901).

[9] It was introduced by the Augustus in the form of the co-regency, for a full discussion of which see Mommsen, *Staatsrecht,* ii. 1145 sqq. (ed. 3).

In the Hellenistic kingdoms (Macedonia, Syria, Egypt) there is material for instructive comparisons in regard to the combination of the elective and dynastic principles, and co-regencies.

[10] This principle was asserted by Andronicus II who endeavoured to exclude his grandson (Andronicus III) from the throne. The civil wars which resulted represent, from the constitutional point of view, a struggle between this principle and the idea of legitimacy to which the Byzantines had become strongly attached.

[11] The regular form of phrase is ἔστεψε διὰ τοῦ Πατριάρχου (cp. Theophanes, 417₂₅, 426₂₇, 480₁₁, 494₂₆). More explicitly Kedrenos ii. 296 ; Romanus I was crowned by the Patriarch ἐπιτροπῇ τοῦ βασιλέως Κωνσταντίνου (who was a minor). In the normal ceremony of crowning a colleague, described in Constantine Porph., *De Cer.,* i. 38, the Patriarch hands the crown to the Emperor, who places it on the new Emperor's head (p. 194).

[12] The colleague is often designated as ὁ δεύτερος βασιλεύς, or as συμβασιλεύς (and we may suppose that the description of Otto II as *co-imperator* of his father was borrowed from this) ; if a child, he is distinguished as " the little Emperor " (ὁ μικρὸς βασιλεύς), and this, no doubt,

explains why Theodosius II was ὁ μικρός. The description, applied to him when a minor, survived his boyhood, because it served to distinguish him from his grandfather and namesake, Theodosius the Great. In one case, we find the term *rex* strangely applied to a second Emperor. It occurs on a bronze coin of the year 866–7, in which Basil I was colleague of Michael III. The obverse has *Mihael imperat(or)*, the reverse *Basilius rex* (Wroth, *Catalogue of the Imperial Byzantine Coins of the British Museum*, ii. 432). I do not know how to explain this eccentricity which is contrary to all the principles of the Roman Imperium. The western title *Romanorum rex*, which in the 11th century began to be assumed by western Emperors before they were crowned at Rome and was afterwards appropriated to their successors, cannot be compared.

[13] *Byzantinische Zeitschrift*, xv. 151 sqq. (1906).

[14] It came into official use in the eleventh century, as a reinforcement of Basileus (β. καὶ αὐτ.), and in Latin diplomas we find it translated by *moderator*, Basileus by *Imperator*. A colleague could only use the title Autokrator by special permission of the senior Emperor (Codinus, *De Officiis*, c. 17, pp. 86, 87, ed. Bonn). But the distinction was drawn as early as the ninth century, for in Philotheos (A.D. 900), *Kletorologion* (*apud* Const. Porph. *De Cerimoniis*, p. 712), we find ὁ αὐτοκράτωρ βασιλεύς explicitly contrasted with ὁ δεύτερος βασιλεύς.

[15] If an Emperor foresaw his approaching death and his colleague was a minor, he could make arrangements for the regency in his will. This was done, e.g., by Theophilus and by Alexander.

[16] Zachariä von Lingenthal, *Jus Graeco-romanum*, iii. 55 (Εἰρήνη πιστὸς βασιλεύς). The point is brought out in the *Chronicle* of Theophanes (p. 466, l. 25, ed. De Boor) : Con-

stantine VI causes the Armeniac soldiers to swear not to accept his mother Irene εἰς βασιλέα. The later force of the term αὐτοκράτωρ comes out in the same passage (l. 15).

[17] In this connexion, however, may be noted the remarkable notion of establishing a democracy, attributed to the Emperor Stauracius (A.D. 811) by the contemporary chronicler Theophanes (ed. De Boor, p. 492). He was on his deathbed at the time and wished to be succeeded by his wife, the Athenian Theophano (a relative of Irene) as sovran Empress. He threatened democracy as an alternative. We should like to know what his idea of a democracy was.

[18] Codinus, *De Officiis*, c. 17.

[19] *Digest*. i. 3. 31 ; *Basilica*, ii. 6. 1.

[20] *Basilica*, ii. 6. 9, καὶ κατὰ βασιλέως οἱ γενικοὶ κρατεί-τωσαν νόμοι καὶ πᾶσα παράνομος ἐκβαλλέσθω ἀντιγραφή. The meaning of *lex generalis* (briefly, an edict promulgated as applicable to the whole Empire) is explained *ib.* 8, which is based on *Cod. Just.* i. 14. 3. The Emperor could not enact a special constitution,—applicable to a section, district, or town,—which was contrary to the provisions of a *lex generalis*.

[21] *Cod. Just.* i. 14. 4, digna vox maiestate regnantis legibus alligatum se principem profiteri : adeo de auctoritate iuris nostra pendet auctoritas.

[22] The functions of the Senate seem to have closely resembled those of the Synedrion in the Hellenistic kingdoms. Compare the account of a meeting of the Synedrion of Antiochus in Polybius, v. 41–42. It may be noticed that during the minority after the death of Romanus II, it is the Senate that appoints Nicephorus II to the supreme command of the Asiatic troops (Leo Diaconus, II. 12). The

importance of the Senate is illustrated by the political
measure of Constantine X who "democratized" it: see
Psellos, *Historia*, p. 238 (ed. Sathas, 1899) ; C. Neumann,
*Die Weltstellung des byzantinischen Reiches vor den
Kreuzzügen*, p. 79.

23 This principle had been already laid down by Justinian
in regard to the first four Councils, the decrees of which he
places on the same level as Holy Scripture: *Nov.* 151, *a'*,
ed. Zachariä, ii. p. 267.

24 The best general account of the relation of State and
Church in Byzantium will be found in the late Professor
Gelzer's article in the *Historische Zeitschrift*, N. F. vol. 50,
193 sqq. (1901). At the Seventh Ecumenical Council
(A.D. 787) the presidency was committed to the Patriarch
Tarasios, evidently because he had been a layman and
minister, not (like most of his predecessors) a monk.

25 Augustinus Triumphus, *Summa de potestate Eccle-
siastica*, I. 1, p. 2, ed. 1584 (Rome): si quis eligatur in
Papam nullum ordinem habens, erit verus Papa et habebit
omnem potestatem iurisdictionis in spiritualibus et tem-
poralibus et tamen nullam habebit potestatem ordinis.

26 *Paraenesis ad Leonem*, in Migne, *Patr. Gr.* cvii.
pp. xxv, xxxii.

27 See Photius, in Migne, *P. G.* cii. 765 and 573.
Cp. Sickel, *op. cit.* 547–8, and on the other hand Brightman, *op. cit.* 383–5.

28 *The Holy Roman Empire* (last ed. 1904), 343 sqq.

29 This is noted by Sidgwick, *Development of European
Polity*, p. 10.

30 For an analysis of the conception of *unconstitutional*
as distinguished from *illegal* see Austin, *op. cit.* 265 sqq.